WONDER®
STARTERS

Spiders

Pictures by RICHARD ORR

Wonder® Books
PRICE/STERN/SLOAN
Publishers, Inc., Los Angeles
1983

About Wonder® Starters

Wonder® Starters are vocabulary controlled information books for young children. More than ninety per cent of the words in the text will be in the reading vocabulary of the vast majority of young readers. Word and sentence length have also been carefully controlled.

Key new words associated with the topic of each book are repeated with picture explanations in the Starters dictionary at the end. The dictionary can also be used as an index for teaching children to look things up.

Teachers and experts have been consulted on the content and accuracy of the books.

Published by Price/Stern/Sloan Publishers, Inc.
410 North La Cienega Boulevard, Los Angeles, California 90048

ISBN: 0-8431-4413-0

I have found a big spider.
It is in the bathtub.

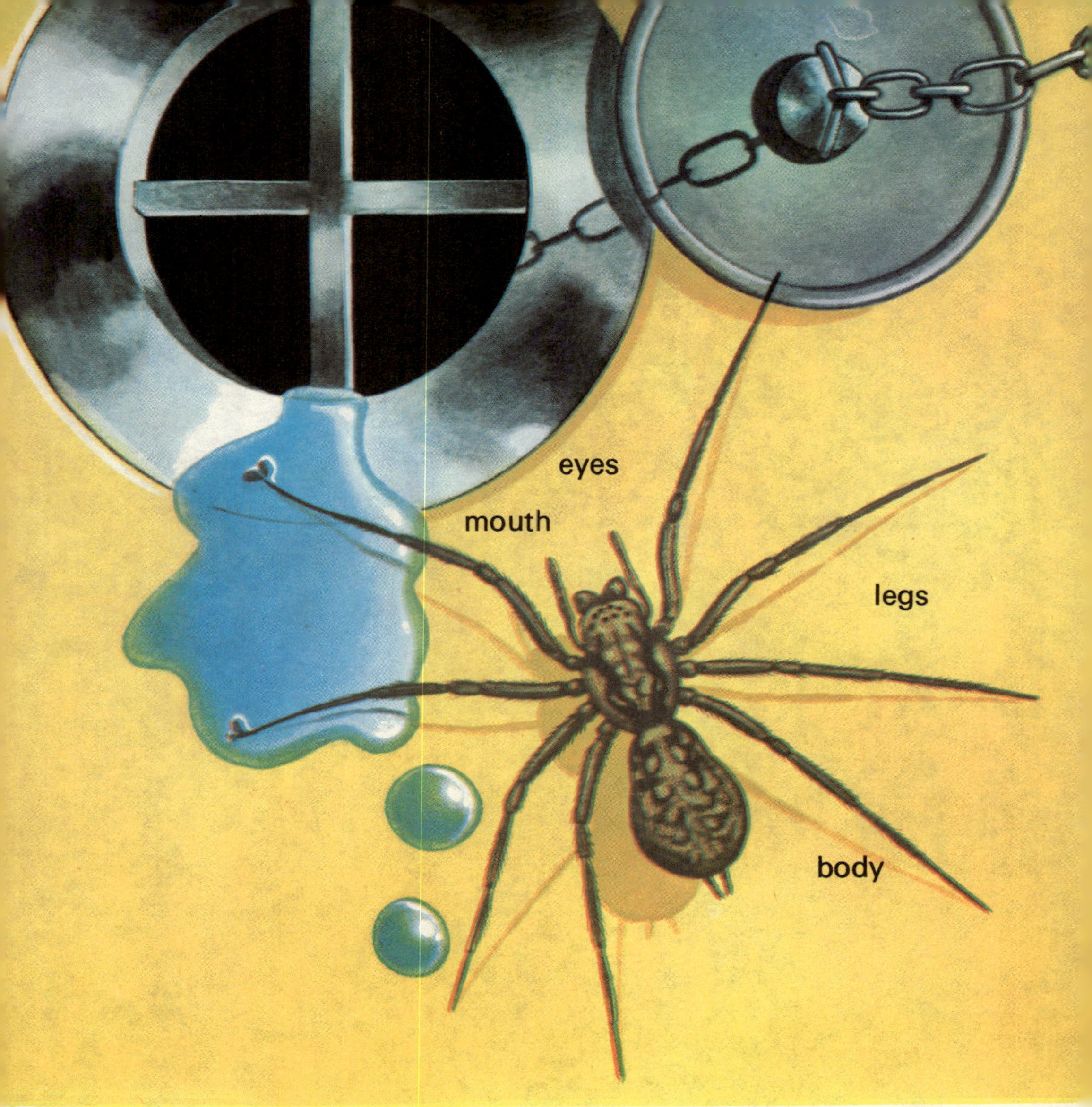

The spider has eight legs.
It has lots of eyes, too.

This spider has made a big web.
It stays on the web, waiting.

A fly has been caught in the web.
The silk threads are sticky.
The fly cannot get away.

Now the spider can eat the fly.
Sometimes spiders wrap flies in silk.
The spider can eat the fly later.

A wasp flies into the web.
Wasps often eat spiders.

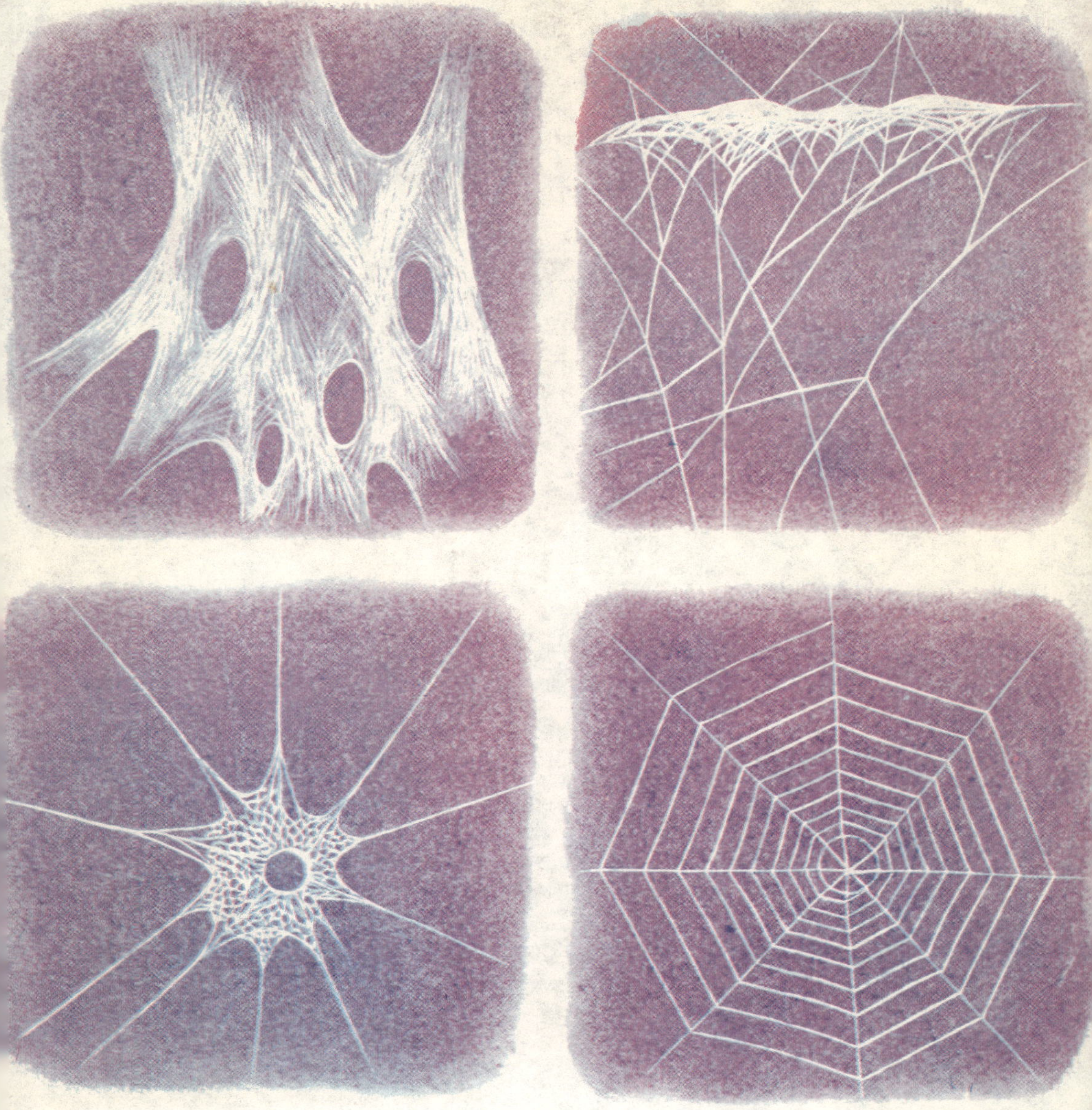

There are lots of different kinds of webs.

Spiders lay eggs.
Sometimes spiders make nests
out of silk.

Some spiders carry their eggs with them.

Baby spiders hatch out of the eggs.
Each baby spins a thread.
The baby spiders hang on to the threads.

The wind blows the baby spiders.
They hang on to their threads.
They fly like balloons.

This spider's leg has broken off.
Now it has only seven legs.
Soon a new leg will grow.

Something has frightened the spider.
It is pretending to be dead.

This spider jumps.
It does not make a web.
The spider jumps on flies
and other insects.

Another spider digs a hole.
It makes a door and lines it with silk.
The spider opens the door
and waits for insects.

Some spiders hide.
Crab spiders sit in flowers.
They make their bodies
the same colors as the flowers.

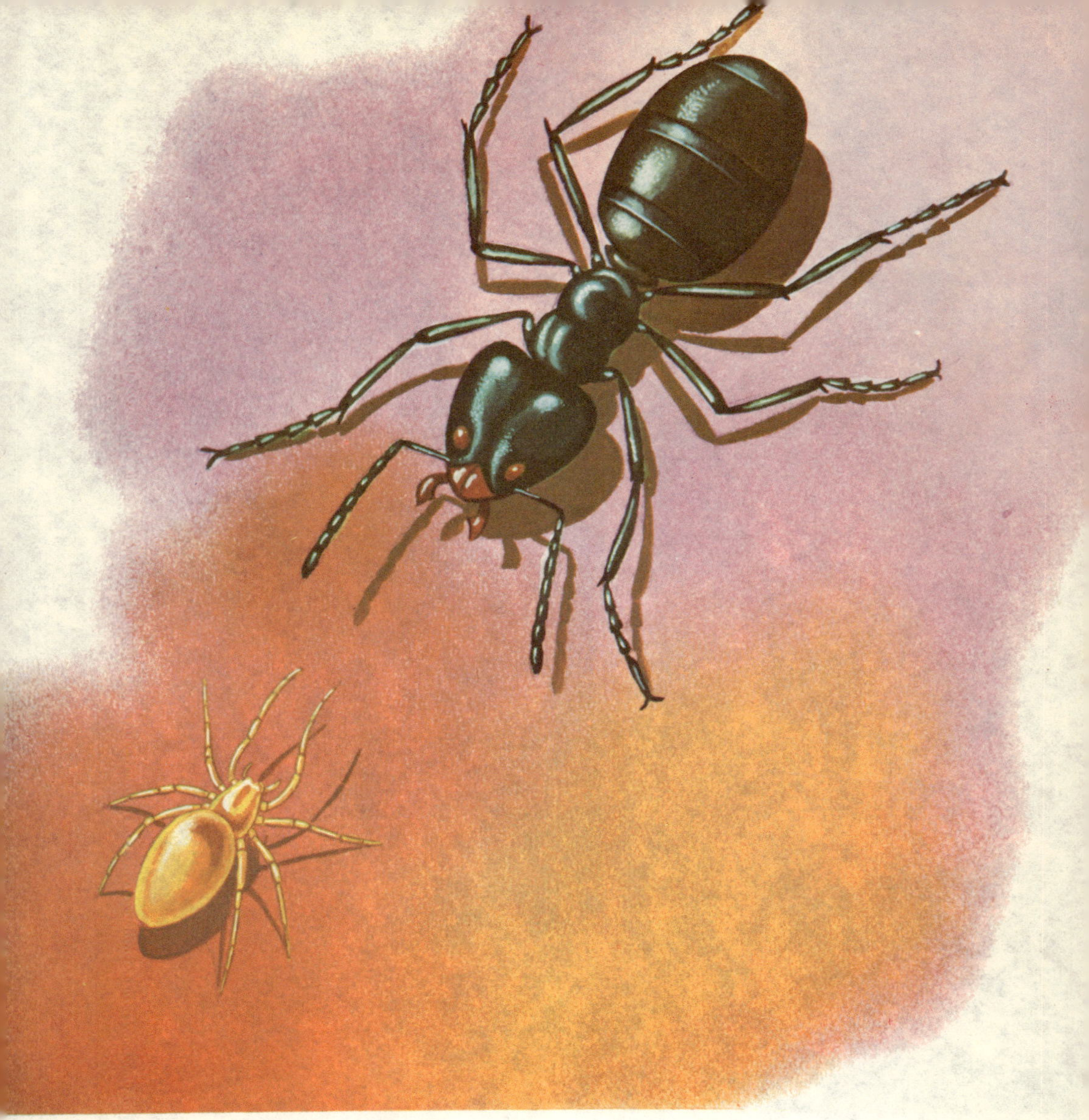

Another spider lives with ants.
It walks on six legs.
It pretends to be an ant.

This is a very big spider.
It can eat birds.

This spider is called a Black Widow.
It is very dangerous.

Some spiders live under water.
They make tents.
They take air into the tent.

A few spiders walk on water.
They hunt for insects and tadpoles.

Some animals eat spiders.
All these animals eat spiders.

Starter's **Spiders** words

bath-
tub
(page 1)

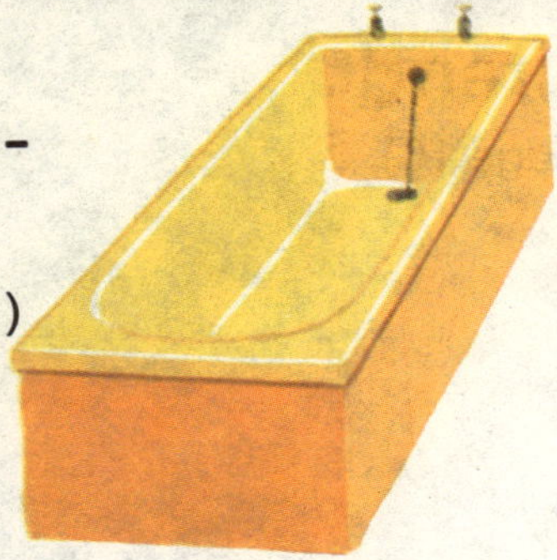

legs
(page 2)

eyes
(page 2)

body
(page 2)

mouth
(page 2)

web
(page 3)

fly
(page 4)

wasp
(page 6)

eggs
(page 8)

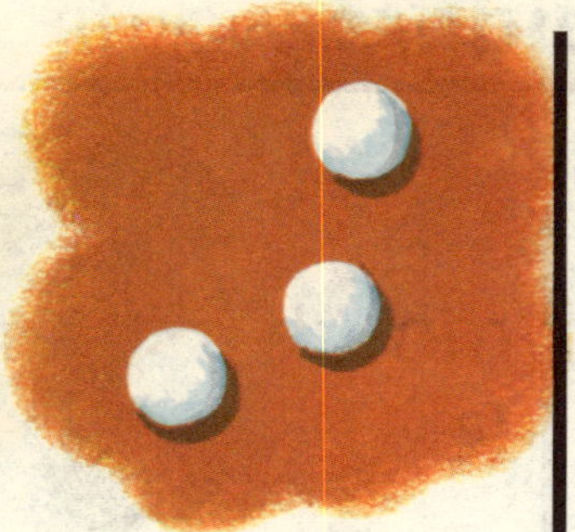

nest
(page 8)

carry
(page 9)

spin
(page 10)

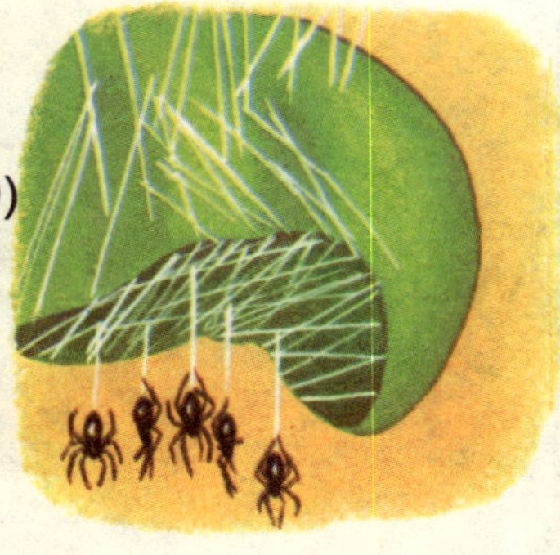

thread
(page 10)

fly
(page 11)

hole
(page 15)

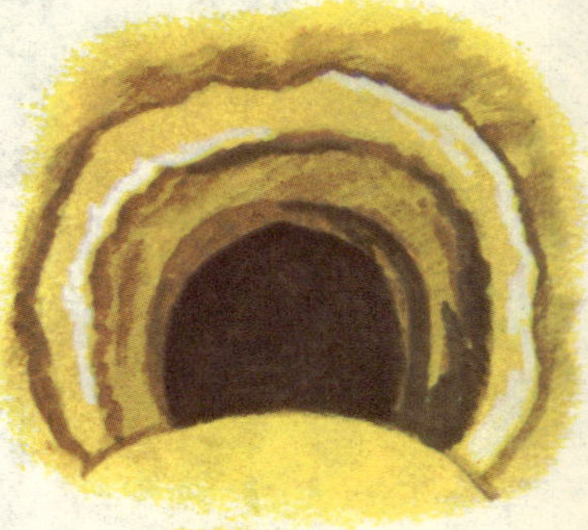

door
(page 15)

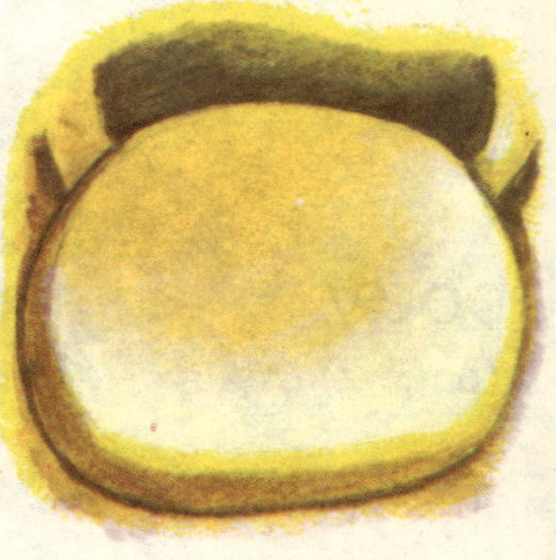

flower
(page 16)

crab
spider
(page 16)

ant
(page 17)

bird
(page 18)

Black
Widow
spider
(page 19)

tent
(page 20)